SUPER SIMPLE
ENGINEERING PROJECTS

ENGINEER IT!
CANAL
PROJECTS

CAROLYN BERNHARDT

CONSULTING EDITOR, DIANE CRAIG, M.A./READING SPECIALIST

Super Sandcastle

An Imprint of Abdo Publishing
abdopublishing.com

abdopublishing.com

Published by Abdo Publishing, a division of ABDO, PO Box 398166, Minneapolis, Minnesota 55439. Copyright © 2018 by Abdo Consulting Group, Inc. International copyrights reserved in all countries. No part of this book may be reproduced in any form without written permission from the publisher. Super SandCastle™ is a trademark and logo of Abdo Publishing.

Printed in the United States of America, North Mankato, Minnesota
062017
092017

THIS BOOK CONTAINS RECYCLED MATERIALS

Production: Mighty Media, Inc.
Editor: Liz Salzmann
Cover Photographs: Mighty Media, Inc.; Shutterstock
Interior Photographs: Mighty Media, Inc.; Shutterstock

The following manufacturers/names appearing in this book are trademarks: LEGO®, Pyrex®, Scotch®, Sharpie®

Publisher's Cataloging-in-Publication Data

Names: Bernhardt, Carolyn, author.
Title: Engineer it! canal projects / by Carolyn Bernhardt.
Other titles: Canal projects
Description: Minneapolis, MN : Abdo Publishing, 2018. | Series: Super simple engineering projects
Identifiers: LCCN 2016963095 | ISBN 9781532111235 (lib. bdg.) | ISBN 9781680789089 (ebook)
Subjects: LCSH: Canals--Juvenile literature. | Canals--Design and construction-- Juvenile literature. | Civil engineering--Juvenile literature.
Classification: DDC 627--dc23
LC record available at http://lccn.loc.gov/2016963095

Super SandCastle™ books are created by a team of professional educators, reading specialists, and content developers around five essential components—phonemic awareness, phonics, vocabulary, text comprehension, and fluency—to assist young readers as they develop reading skills and strategies and increase their general knowledge. All books are written, reviewed, and leveled for guided reading and early reading intervention programs for use in shared, guided, and independent reading and writing activities to support a balanced approach to literacy instruction.

TO ADULT HELPERS

The projects in this title are fun and simple. There are just a few things to remember. Some projects require the use of sharp objects. Also, kids may be using messy materials such as glue or paint. Make sure they protect their clothes and work surfaces. Review the projects before starting, and be ready to assist when necessary.

KEY SYMBOL

Watch for this warning symbol in this book. Here is what it means.

SHARP! You will be working with a sharp object. Get help!

CONTENTS

WHAT IS A CANAL

A canal is a human-made river. Canals are used to move goods and people. Most canals connect two bodies of water.

Canals were particularly important before trains, cars, and airplanes were invented. People had to use animals to carry or pull goods over land. This was slow and hard to do, especially if there were mountains in the way. Canals provided easier routes for **transportation**.

PACKHORSES

CANAL

THE ERIE CANAL

The first major canal built in the United States was the Erie Canal. It was completed in 1825. The Erie Canal crosses New York between the Hudson River and Lake Erie. It was one of the few ways to get past the Appalachian Mountains. The Erie Canal made **transportation** from the East Coast to the Midwest much easier. As a result, communities and trade west of the mountains quickly increased.

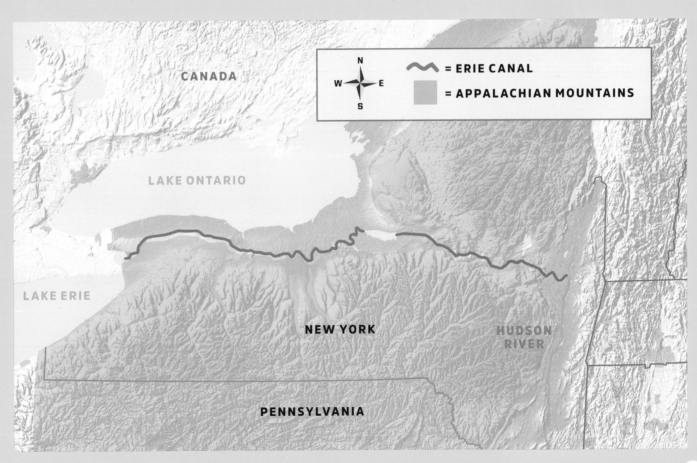

= ERIE CANAL

= APPALACHIAN MOUNTAINS

CANADA

LAKE ONTARIO

LAKE ERIE

NEW YORK

HUDSON RIVER

PENNSYLVANIA

HOW PEOPLE
USE CANALS

Canals can have many uses. These include moving people and goods, watering crops, and helping control floods.

SHIPPING

Huge ships can travel through large canals, such as the Suez Canal in Egypt. Canals help these ships move goods around the world.

TRAVEL

In some places, canals are like city streets. Venice, Italy, has canals like this. People use boats to get around town.

IRRIGATION

The oldest canals in the world were used for irrigation. Farmers used the canal water to water their crops. There are still many irrigation canals in use today.

FLOOD CONTROL

Floodgates control the water level in a canal. During a storm, more water can be kept in the canal. Then it doesn't flood nearby areas.

CANAL LOCKS

Some canals flow up or down hills. These canals have one or more locks that allow ships to change levels.

A lock is an enclosed section of a canal. To go up or down a level, the boat enters an enclosed section of the canal. The lock closes behind the boat. Then the water level in the lock is raised or lowered. When the water level matches the level in the canal, the front of the lock opens. The boat leaves the lock and continues along the canal.

THE PANAMA CANAL

The Panama Canal opened in 1914. It is 50 miles (80 km) long. The canal is in Panama, a country on the southern tip of Central America. Ships use this canal to travel between the Atlantic and Pacific Oceans. Before the canal opened, ships had to travel around South America. The canal shortened the trip by thousands of miles.

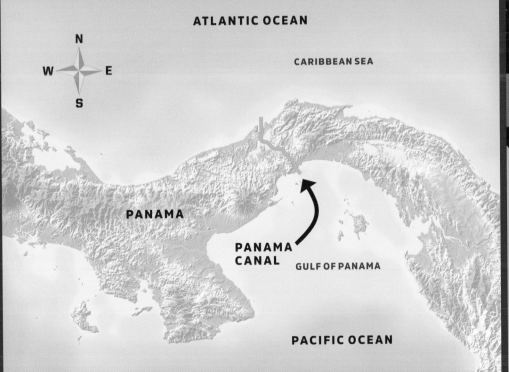

ATLANTIC OCEAN

N
W   E
S

CARIBBEAN SEA

PANAMA

PANAMA
CANAL

GULF OF PANAMA

PACIFIC OCEAN

UNITED
STATES

ATLANTIC
OCEAN

PANAMA

SOUTH
AMERICA

PACIFIC
OCEAN

MATERIALS

Here are some of the materials that you will need for the projects in this book.

ALUMINUM PAN   CARDBOARD   CLAY   CRAFT FOAM   CRAFT KNIFE   DOUBLE-SIDED TAPE

DUCT TAPE   EYE DROPPER   FELT   FOAM TUBING   FUNNEL   HOLE PUNCH

 HOOK-AND-LOOP TAPE

 LEGO BASES AND BLOCKS

 MEASURING CUPS

 PAINT

 PAINTBRUSHES

 PAPER FASTENERS

 PITCHER

 PLASTIC BIN

 PLASTIC BOTTLE

 PLASTIC CUP

 PLASTIC PLATE

 PONY BEADS

 PUSHPINS

 SAND

 SUPER-STRONG MAGNETS

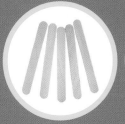 TOOTHPICK

 WOODEN CRAFT STICKS

 WOODEN SKEWERS

CLAY
CANAL CARVING

MATERIALS: paper, scissors, plastic plate, pencil, clay, wooden skewer, drinking glass, water, eye dropper

A canal usually has a water source. This is a natural body of water, such as an ocean or a lake. The canal takes water from the source to other areas where it is needed.

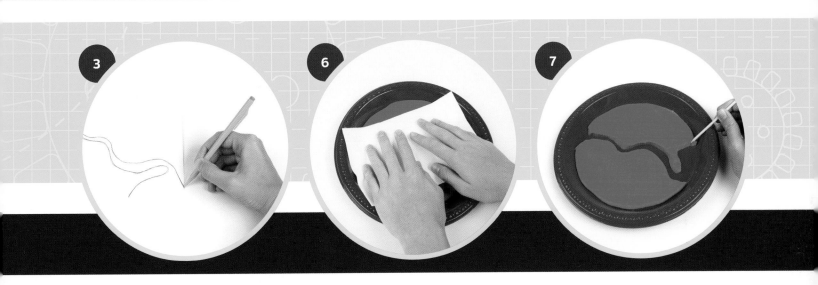

① Have an adult help you **research** canals **online**. Look at some maps of canals to get inspired!

② Cut a piece of paper so it is about the size of the plastic plate.

③ Draw a canal on the paper with a pencil. Be sure to include a water source at one end.

④ Trace over the drawing a few times to make the lines really dark.

⑤ Press a layer of clay in the bottom of the plate.

⑥ Press the drawing facedown on the clay. Remove the drawing. The marks from your pencil should show up clearly on the clay.

⑦ Use a wooden skewer to carve your canal into the clay. Follow the lines from your drawing.

⑧ Fill the glass with water. Use an eyedropper to drop water in the water source. Watch as the canal allows the water to flow from the water source to other parts of the map!

LEGO WATER
TRACK

MATERIALS: LEGO pieces, large LEGO base, small LEGO base, plastic bin, measuring cup, water

A canal is carefully **designed** for its location and purpose. Engineers have to figure out the best way to move water and boats from one place to another.

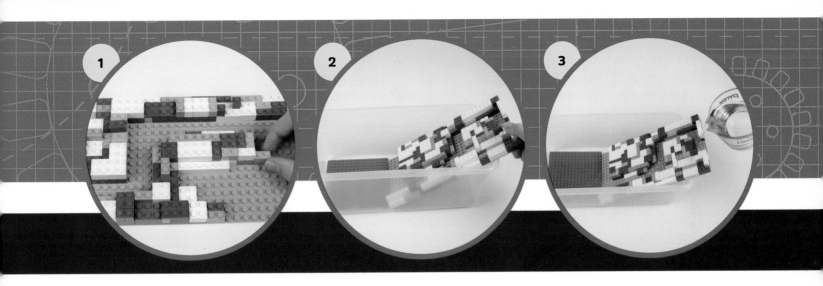

1 Use LEGO pieces to build a canal on the large LEGO base. Press the LEGO pieces firmly against the base.

2 Use a smaller LEGO base to hold the canal at an angle in the plastic bin.

3 Fill the measuring cup with water. Pour water into the top of the canal.

4 Watch the water flow through the canal you created.

5 Break your canal down and try other canal **designs**. See how the flow of the water changes.

CANAL SHAPE
SHUFFLE

MATERIALS: cardboard, ruler, scissors, felt, double-sided tape, paper, pencil, hook-and-loop tape

Canals are sometimes built in **wetlands** or areas with many small lakes. The canals connect these bodies of water. Then people can use the canals to travel throughout the area.

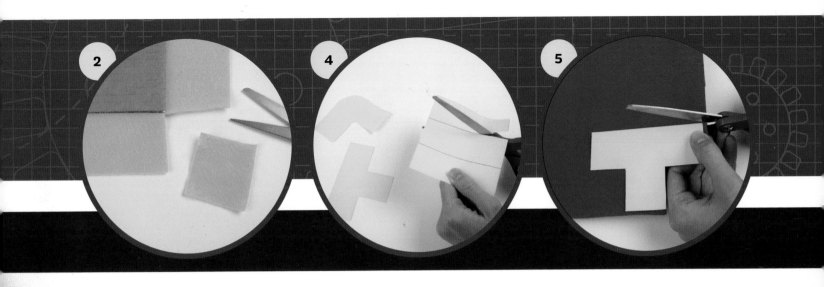

① Cut a cardboard rectangle that is 20 by 12 inches (51 by 30 cm). Cut a piece of felt a little bigger than the cardboard.

② Lay the cardboard on the felt. Cut a square out of each corner of the felt.

③ Put double-sided tape along the edges of the felt. Fold the felt over the edges of the cardboard. Turn the board over.

④ Draw canal puzzle pieces on paper. Draw a *T* shape, a straight piece, and a corner piece. Make them all the same width but different lengths. Cut out the pieces.

⑤ Use the paper shapes to cut canal pieces out of felt. Cut out several of each shape.

⑥ Cut trees, buildings, boats, and bridges out of felt.

Continued on the next page.

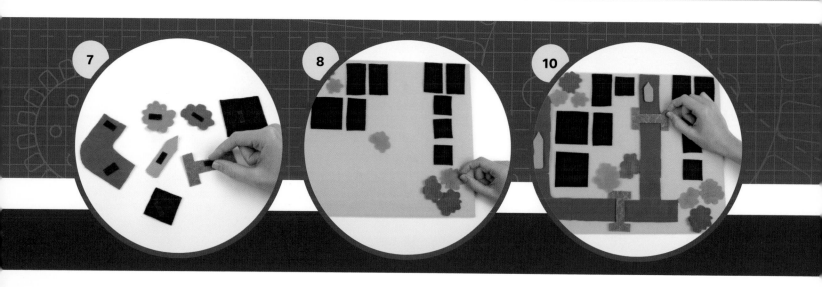

CANAL SHAPE SHUFFLE (CONTINUED)

⑦ Stick pieces of scratchy hook-and-loop tape to the backs of the felt shapes.

⑧ Arrange the trees and buildings on the felt board.

⑨ Add the canal. Have it wind around the **obstacles** you made out of the trees and buildings.

⑩ Add bridges and boats.

⑪ Remove everything and try different arrangements. Cut out more shapes as needed.

DIGGING DEEPER

One area with many canals is the **wetlands** along the coast of Louisiana. The wetland is a large **delta** where the Mississippi River flows into the Gulf of Mexico. In the 1930s, companies started logging trees and drilling for oil in the wetlands. They built bigger canals to move large ships and supplies through the wetlands to the gulf.

These straight, deep, and wide canals are helpful for business. But they are destroying the wetlands. Many people are working to find ways to preserve the wetlands along the Louisiana coast.

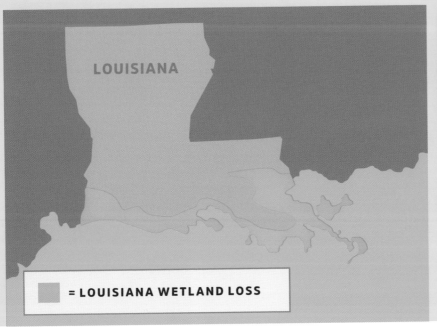

LOUISIANA

■ = LOUISIANA WETLAND LOSS

UNITED STATES

LOUISIANA

N
W E
S

EROSION
SHIELD

MATERIALS: aluminum pan, sand, rocks, measuring cup, cardboard, ruler, scissors, duct tape, pitcher, water

The water in a canal can carve into the land. The water pulls dirt and sand away from the shoreline. This is called erosion. To prevent erosion, some canals are lined with erosion shields. The shields are usually made of gravel, stone, or concrete.

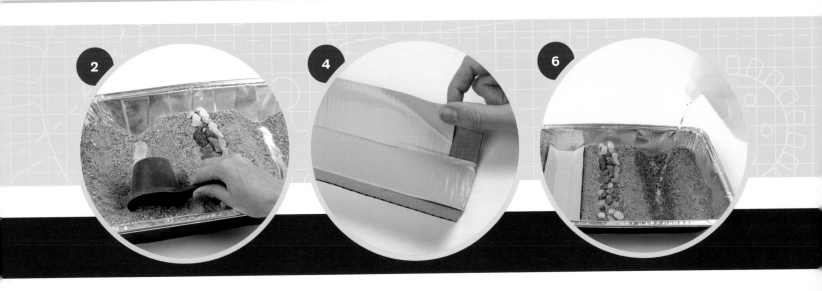

① Fill the pan one-fourth full of sand. Arrange rocks in a line across the middle of the pan.

② Carve a canal on each side of the rock line with the measuring cup. Scoop that sand back out of the pan.

③ Cut a strip of cardboard that is about 6 inches (15 cm) wide. Make it as long as the width of the pan.

④ Fold the strip in thirds **lengthwise**. Unfold the strip and cover it with duct tape. This is the erosion shield.

⑤ Place the erosion shield in one of the canals.

⑥ Pour water into the canal without a shield. What happens to the shape of the canal?

⑦ Pour water into the erosion shield. What happens to the shape of the canal?

FALKIRK
WHEEL REPLICA

MATERIALS: cardboard, marker, plastic bottle, scissors, newspaper, paint, paintbrush, pushpin, wooden skewer, ruler, duct tape, hole punch, 2 paper fasteners, 2 pony beads, craft knife, funnel, plastic cup, sand, foam tubing

A canal can have changing water levels. Boats that travel through canals need to be able to **navigate** these changes easily. One way to do this is with a system of locks. Another way is with special boat lifts. The lifts raise and lower boats as the level of the canal changes. One famous boat lift is the Falkirk Wheel in Scotland.

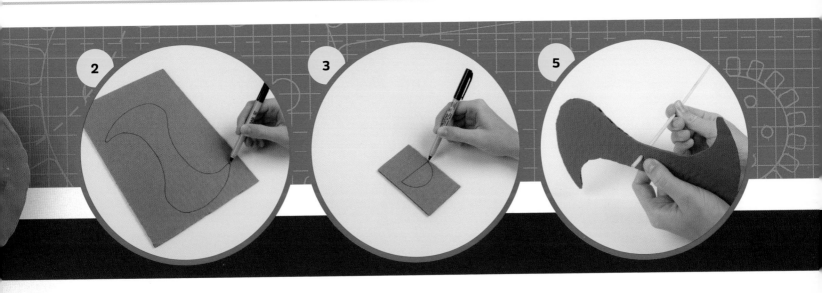

① Read about the Falkirk Wheel on page 25.

② Draw the shape of the wheel on a piece of cardboard. Make it a little longer than the height of the plastic bottle.

③ Draw two half-circles on cardboard. Make them smaller than the wide areas of the wheel. These half-circles are the gondolas.

④ Cut out the wheel and gondolas. Cover your work surface with newspaper. Paint the wheel and gondolas. Let the paint dry.

⑤ Make a hole in the center of the wheel with a pushpin. Push the wooden skewer through the hole. One end should stick out about 1 inch (2.5 cm). Tape the skewer in place. The long end is the wheel's **axle**.

Continued on the next page.

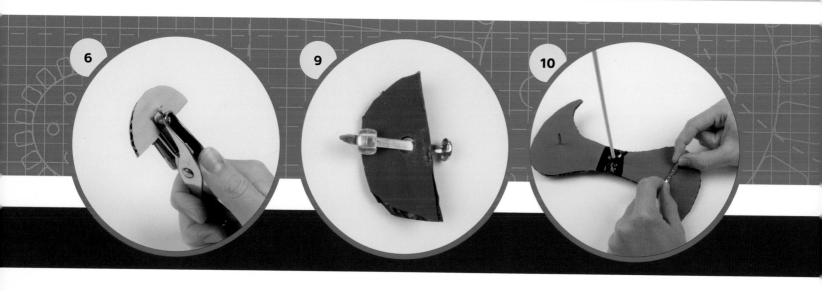

6 Punch a hole through each gondola near its straight edge.

7 Lay the wheel down with the **axle** pointing up. Set a gondola in the center of each end of the wheel. Make marks on the wheel through the holes in the gondolas.

8 Use the pushpin to make a hole in the wheel at each mark.

9 Put a paper fastener through the hole in each gondola. Put a bead on each paper fastener. Push the beads up to the cardboard.

10 Push the fasteners through the holes in the wheel. Separate the ends of the fasteners to hold them in place.

11 Carefully use a craft knife to cut a small X near the top of the bottle. Cut another X across from the first one.

12 Fill the bottle halfway with sand.

13 Push the **axle** through the holes in the bottle.

14 Cut a 6-inch (15 cm) piece of foam tubing in half **lengthwise**. Place one half on top of the bottle. Place the other at the bottom of the bottle. These are the upper and lower channels.

DIGGING DEEPER

The Falkirk Wheel is like a **Ferris wheel** for boats. It is a rotating boat lift. There is a **container** called a gondola on each end of the wheel. A boat enters a gondola. Then the wheel turns. This moves the boat to the other section of the canal.

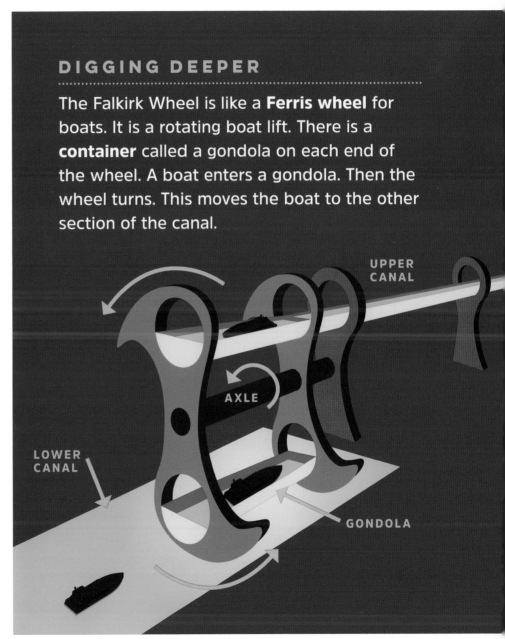

UPPER CANAL

AXLE

LOWER CANAL

GONDOLA

CANAL
NAVIGATION

MATERIALS: craft foam, scissors, plastic bin, foam tubing, duct tape, 2 drinking glasses, plastic cup, water, craft glue, 2 small super-strong magnets, toothpick, double-sided tape, wooden craft stick

Canals can include **obstacles** to get past. It takes skill and experience for a boater to successfully make his or her way through a canal!

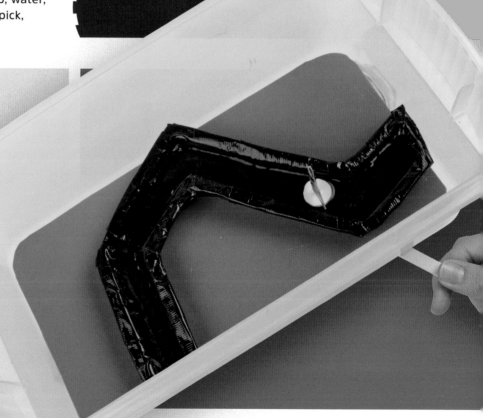

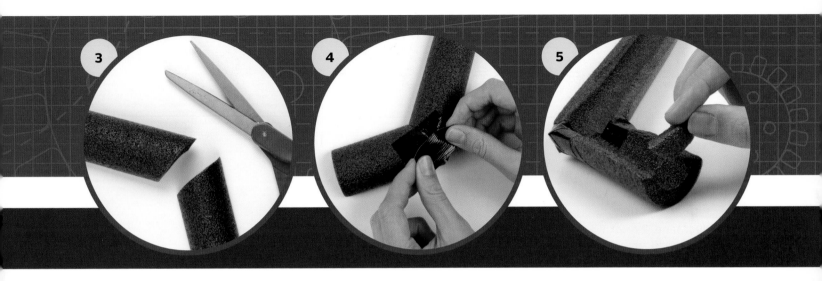

① Cut a piece of green craft foam that fits in the bottom of the bin.

② Carefully cut the foam tubing in half **lengthwise**.

③ **Design** a canal that fits in the plastic bin. Cut pieces of tubing to fit your design. Make corners by cutting the ends at an angle.

④ Tape the pieces together with duct tape.

⑤ Close off the ends of the canal. Cut two small half-circles out of leftover tubing. Make sure they fit in the ends of the canal. Tape them in place.

⑥ Cover the canal with duct tape. Place it in the bin.

Continued on the next page.

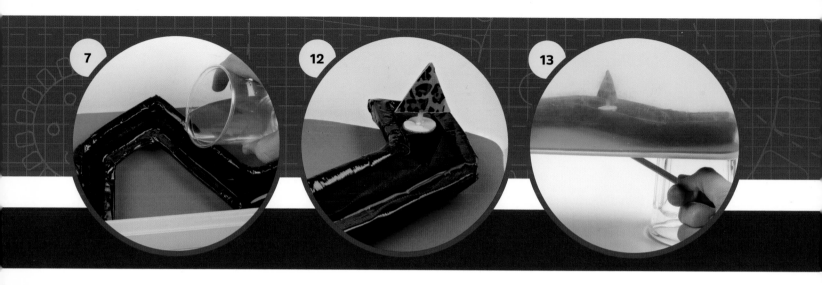

CANAL NAVIGATION (CONTINUED)

⑦ Set the glasses next to each other. Place the bin on top of the glasses. Fill the canal with water.

⑧ Cut a small circle out of craft foam. Glue it to a magnet. This is the hull of your boat.

⑨ Cut two small triangles out of craft foam. Glue them together with one end of the toothpick between them.

⑩ Poke the other end of the toothpick into the middle of the boat's hull. Glue it in place. Let the glue dry.

⑪ Tape the second magnet to the end of a craft stick.

⑫ Put the boat at one end of the canal.

⑬ Hold the magnet on the craft stick under the bin. Use it to pull your boat along the canal.

DIGGING DEEPER

Many different kinds of boats use canals. Some are even **designed** just for use on canals. One of these is the narrowboat. Narrowboats are built for canals in England. Some of the locks on these canals are only 7 feet (2 m) wide. So, any boat that needs to use the locks must be narrower than that. Originally, narrowboats carried goods. Today, they are mostly used for personal travel. Some people even live on them!

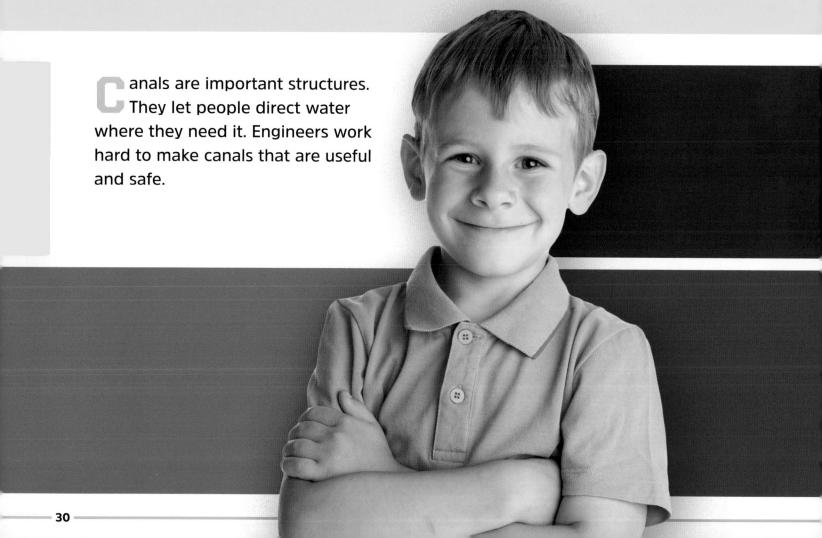

CONCLUSION

Canals are important structures. They let people direct water where they need it. Engineers work hard to make canals that are useful and safe.

QUIZ

1. A canal is a human-made river.
   TRUE OR FALSE?

2. How long is the Panama Canal?

3. What are canals in Louisiana destroying?

LEARN MORE ABOUT IT!

You can find out more about canals all over the world at the library.
Or you can ask an adult to help you **research** canals **online**.

Answers: 1. True 2. 50 miles (80 km) 3. Wetlands

GLOSSARY

axle – a bar that connects two wheels.

container – something that other things can be put into.

delta – an area of land where a river spreads out before entering the sea.

design – 1. the appearance or style of something. 2. to plan how something will appear or work.

Ferris wheel – an amusement ride that has a large vertical wheel with seats around its edge.

lengthwise – in the direction of the longest side.

navigate – to find the way over, across, or through something.

obstacle – something that you have to go over or around.

online – connected to the Internet.

research – to find out more about something.

transportation – the act of moving people and things.

wetland – a low, wet area of land such as a swamp or a marsh.